WORSHIP

THAT'S WHY WE ARE HERE

Worship is like a seed.
Creates and produces an output—
A place of habitation,
A delightful place,
Where we can walk with Light
In Light,
And speaks **with** Truth
In truth.

Scripture Quotations

Unless otherwise indicated, all Scripture quotations in this volume are taken from the King James Version (KJV) of the Bible.

Disclaimer

This book is intended for inspirational and devotional purposes only. It is not a substitute for professional counseling, pastoral guidance, or theological study. The author and publisher make no guarantees regarding spiritual or personal outcomes.

Cover & Interior Design: Adrienne Randle, byadrienne.com

ISBN 979-8-9947399-0-7

Printed in USA

For permissions, inquiries, or bulk purchases, please contact:

www.worshipwhy.com
https://www.youtube.com/@WorshipWhy
info@worshipwhy.com

SPECIAL THANKS

With gratitude to Pastor Christine Hubbard, whose invitation to speak in a moment of transition became a catalyst for the season in which these reflections were formed.

Introduction

During a Sunday service, as the congregation settled in, one of my roles was to start the only video we had purchased—an Easter video titled The Resurrection Means Everything.

One day, the computer malfunctioned, and the video wouldn't play. The Pastor asked me to "have words" instead. Have words? I thought. I love the Lord, I thank the Lord—but impromptu words? From that day forward, she retired the video.

From a spiritual perspective, this assignment became one of the greatest blessings in my life. Only the Lord knew that moment would start me on a journey of keeping my mind truly focused on Him. He knew the challenges that lay ahead in the years to come—challenges that would require stability and peace.

I began listening for the Lord's voice, capturing words and phrases that brought inspiration throughout the week. On Saturdays and early Sunday mornings, I would ask the Lord to shape that week's message.

Though this work was first spoken in communal worship spaces, it is not confined to a church setting. "Why We Are Here" ultimately points beyond a gathering—to a calling. This journal explores why we are here on earth: to worship, to align, to respond, and to live awake to God.

Each entry is intentionally shaped for the page—meant to be read slowly, received prayerfully, and carried into worship rather than hurried through as instruction.

These inspirations, now formed into a journal, lead readers through a journey of faith, reflection, and worship, touching themes of belief, redemption, provision, surrender, gratitude, relationship, and growth.

As Jesus reminds us in John 4:23–24, "But the hour cometh, and now is, when the true worshippers shall worship the Father in spirit and in truth: for the Father seeketh such to worship him. God is a Spirit: and they that worship him must worship him in spirit and in truth."

Reflection

After each worship prose, you are invited to reflect, connect, and engage with your spiritual journey freely, and without pressure to perform. Through guided prompts, discover how God's presence moves in your life, and use journaling to create a personal dialogue with Him.

Table of Contents

Praise & Worship

Responding to God from remembrance, reverence, and trust

- Seeking After God
- He Knows, and He Holds
- His Testimonies Are Sure!
- Wonder How I Got Over?
- Oh, That Men Will Praise Him

Reflection & Gratitude

Honoring what God has done and preparing to pour back out

- Look Back Praise
- Merciful God
- His Universe
- The Thicket of Flesh
- God of Comfort
- Watered Garden
- Ready to Release and Unleash

Entering Worship

I come now to worship.

Not to perform.
Not to ask.
But to behold.

I usher in Your presence—
not with sound,
but with a surrendered heart.

I set the atmosphere within my spirit
so it is conducive to worship.

I turn off the mental burners—
the thoughts simmering,
the concerns boiling over—
anything that interferes with reverence.

I turn my attention fully to You.

There is no music guiding me—
only the melody of my heart.

I come postured in humility,
resting in the confidence
that You have the answers.

You are light.
I take a spiritual walk with You.

Lord, I honor You for who You are.

You are sovereign.
Alpha and Omega.
The beginning and the end.

You chose this generation
for me to exist with You.

You are aware.
You are present.

You are a great and magnificent God—
my strength,

my power.

You created the heavens
and stretched them out.

You formed the earth
and spread it abroad.

You made me a living soul.

And now my eyes can behold Your essence,
and my spirit can house Your presence.

You already know the truth—
because You are Truth.

In this moment,
I speak to You the truths of my heart.

I permit You
to deposit a healing balm.

I find solace in knowing
I have an expected end.

I listen now—
not for noise,
but for instruction.

Instruction that leads me
to walk in obedience. Yes.

Lord, I bring one sacred request:
Create in me a clean heart.
Renew a right spirit within me.

That I may remain a vessel,
a light,
a witness—
for Your name's sake.

And now, Lord... I wait.

Invitation & Alignment

*A gentle call to awaken the heart, realign the soul, and enter
worship with intention, truth, and readiness.*

From this place of stillness, we now turn to the question.

Worship has a way of quieting what is loud
and revealing what is true.

From that place, the question can finally be heard.

The Question Is

The Answer Is:
The tomb is empty—

The Question Is:
Has He risen in our lives,
or is He still only alive in our language?

We are here because a resurrected King
has called forth a resurrected people—
a people who are not waiting for revival,
but who realize: we are the revival.

Christianity is not a costume.
Not a borrowed phrase.
Not an accessory.

It is rebirth—
the old self, set aside.
A crossing over into a new kingdom.
A transformation.
A privilege—access to the manifold wisdom of God.

It is a renewed mind.
A life aligned with the Spirit.
Christ was both obedience to the cross
and became the sacrifice.

Our sacrifice and obedience?
To fortify ourselves.
To mortify the deeds of the flesh.

We are here with intent—
to walk in power,
to speak with purpose,
to fortify,
in order to modify the deeds of this flesh.

The Reality Is:
Every time we open our mouth,
we release something.
The Question Is:
Does it sound like Him?

We are here to be aligned—
mind, body, soul, and spirit.
To remember where we belong.
To reflect the sound of this Kingdom.

Not tossed.
Not teetering.
But rooted—to root out.
Built—to build up.
Unshaken and always abounding.

The Answer Is:
We were bought with Blood—the sacrifice that secured our redemption and freedom.
We are a purchased possession,
sealed with the Spirit of promise.

The Question Is:
When we rise with Him,
when we walk as He walked,
and love as He loved—

Will we follow Him?
Will we lay down our lives daily?
Will we rise fully?

Let us not lose track
of where the Spirit is leading.
Let us not lose sight
of where the Spirit is moving.

We are here for:
His Name.
His Praise.
His Glory.

The Final Question Is:
Will we hear?

We are here to echo resurrection
until every dry bone hears:
Live.
Rise.
Take up your bed and walk.

That's why we are here.

Created to Worship

Because our walk and our praise are not mechanical,
no warm-ups are required.
No batteries.
No cranking.

Understanding is required.

We were made to be worshipers.

Praise is comely for the upright.

We are settled in this truth:
though there are many devices in the heart of man,
the counsel of the Lord shall prevail.

We also understand the need to travel light.
We cannot take everything with us.
We cannot take everyone with us.
Worship clarifies what stays and what must be released.

Our walk and our praise are voice-activated.
The answer of the mouth, spoken rightly, produces joy.
We declare what He has already spoken.
We command dry bones to live again.

We are here as lively stones,
growing in understanding,
lifting praise,
and speaking into the atmosphere.

It is showtime.

The Lord did not bring us here to leave us hanging.
He will show Himself strong on our behalf.

He desires to put His glory on display.
He has ushered in a cloud of witnesses— an audience
to see faith lived out and glory revealed,
to see us clothed in strength and honor,
and for us to witness Him confuse and scatter our enemies.

We praise Him in advance
for the victory released through His glory and power.

Because we believed,
because we fasted,

because we prayed—
a shift occurred.

That shift may have caused a rift,
but His right hand upheld us,
and His gentleness made us great.

We were created to worship—
not from effort,
but from understanding.

And as we believed,
as we prayed,
as we trusted and obeyed,
He fulfilled His Word
and brought us into a wealthy place.

THAT'S WHY WE ARE HERE

Reflection

Created to Worship

Journal:

Write a few lines of praise declaring who God is to you right now.
Note one way you can use your voice this week to honor Him — through
prayer, declaration, or gratitude.

Scriptures:

John 4:23–24
Psalm 100:2
Psalm 34:1

The Profit is in the Yes!

Therefore, in the midst of temptations and distractions,
you have fixed your focus on Christ and the power of His sacrifice.

- Your spirit got clocked on steadfast
- Your heart and mind joined in

Now, having the power to overpower your own will,
we are here in this glorified state
to abound in the work of the Lord.

Because in all His splendor, greatness, power, glory, victory, and majesty,
He is the only One who can truly blow our minds and take us on a journey
to tap into the breadth, length, depth, heights, the fullness,
and the vastness of God.

We are here to go on a spiritual journey, camp out in wealthy places,
and become students of spiritual authority.

We are here to declare God's glory
and exalt the name of Him who is Head above all.

Because He has the "know-how."
Therefore, He can fix it.

We are here to quiet our spirit
and hear what thus saith the Lord.

Because we do not belong in low places.
That is not the rightful position.
A life estate there - a place never meant to be home - is not written that way in His
will; therefore,

He went down into the abyss of our souls,
and by His knowledge the depths were broken up;
the clouds dropped down the dew.

He began excavating the life-threatening issues.
He followed it with a heart operation.
He ministered to our needs.

He is so skillful,
He was careful not to leave the enemy stitched inside.

He led us out on the long, continuous path called perfect peace.
He gave us simple maintainability instructions:
"Keep your mind stayed on Me."

We are here to seek instruction
so we are not misguided in our thoughts or our responses.

Because now we can see.

The reality is coming into view.

The Scriptures are full
and ready to be fulfilled.

We cannot take things with us.
Only what we do for Christ will last.
To live is Christ; to die is gain.

Since the profit is in the yes,
we are here to do the work of the Lord
while we are under the umbrella of while.

THAT'S WHY WE ARE HERE

Reflection

The Profit Is in the YES

Journal:

Write a prayer placing a current challenge or concern into God's hands.

Acknowledge where He has already begun healing, restoring, or realigning your life, and choose to trust His "know-how" over your own understanding.

Scripture:

2 Corinthians 1:20

Worship — A Place of Habitation

From the beginning, God ordained that through the birth, crucifixion,
death, burial, resurrection, and ascension of Jesus Christ,
He would become both Lord and Savior.

He dismantled the middle wall of separation
that would have confined us to perdition.
He became the Great Reconciler,
restoring contaminated humanity back to God
and extending a true right hand of fellowship.

He purified a people unto Himself.

Worship is no longer ritual.
It is relationship.
No longer self-righteous effort,
but the righteousness of God.

Now, as those who are
no longer enslaved to sin,
no longer stalled in indecision,
no longer toiling but gathering,
no longer governed by the flesh but growing strong in spirit—
we stand as trees of righteousness,

clapping our branches in rejoicing,
proclaiming the praises of Him
who called us out of darkness
into marvelous light.

We walk circumspectly, knowing we are sojourners.
This world is not our home.
What we see is temporary,
mortal,
corruptible,
and fading.

But the Word of the Lord is incorruptible.
We are sealed with the Holy Spirit of promise.
And when He returns,
mortality will give way to immortality,
corruption to incorruption—
in a moment,
in the twinkling of an eye.

This is not the hour to cast away faith
or surrender confidence.
Those who endure will receive the reward.

We worship because worship is like a seed.
It produces.
It creates a place of habitation—
a delightful place
where our spirit walks with Light in light
and speaks with Truth in truth.

We are here to talk with God.
To be strengthened.
To be built up through worship.
To declare what He has done for our souls.

When life came apart at the seams,
He kept us standing.
When our plans shattered,
He gathered the pieces
and made us whole—
nothing missing, nothing broken.

We worship because worship is a place of habitation.

Amid confusion and noise,
He painted peace with His rod and staff.
Green pastures appeared.
Still waters flowed.
Streams of living water diversified our steps.
He set us on the path to a wealthy place.

So we declare in worship: *The Lord is my Shepherd. I have everything I need.*

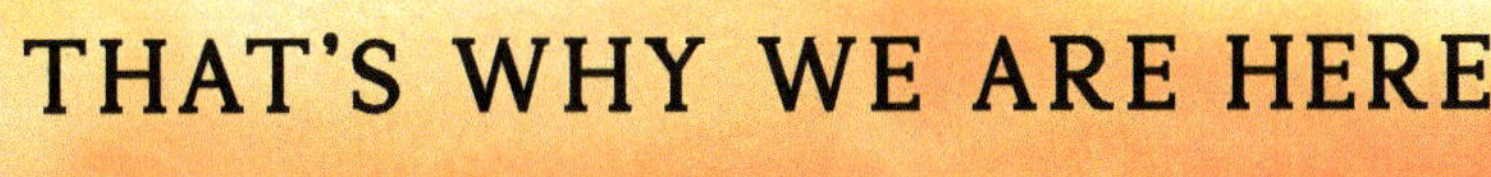

Reflection

Worship: A Place of Habitation

Journal:

Write a short prayer inviting God to make your worship a place He inhabits.

Note one way your daily life can reflect worship beyond music or words.

Scriptures:

John 4:23–24
Psalm 22:3

God Is in the Midst

Known unto God are all His works
and all His people.

We are here to let Him know
we remember His deeds
and are thankful.

Because grace and mercy
have been quietly surrounding loved ones
who have not yet come
into the knowledge of the truth,
we are here to offer
a prayer of thanksgiving
for the changes now unfolding.

Because when we came
to a fork in the road
on Major Decision Boulevard
and did not know which way to go,
we called on His name
and received sudden peace,
strength, and direction.

We are here to thank Him
for insight, revelation,
and guidance.

Because He has attended
to the voice of our prayers
and granted the petitions
of our hearts,
we are here to make His deeds known
and to express hearts
full of thanksgiving.

THAT'S WHY WE ARE HERE

Reflection

God Is in the Midst

Journal:

Where have you seen God quietly at work, even before you fully recognized it?

What vows, prayers, or promises did you speak during a difficult season that now deserve thanksgiving?

Scriptures:

Psalm 66:20
Proverbs 3:6

Redemption, Promise & Relationship

Reflections that ground identity in redemption, strengthen trust in God's promises, and deepen relationship through surrender and belief.

We Only Get One of These

Because there is so much more before us,

more opportunity,
more praise,
more manifestation,
more glory,
more power,
more revelation
from the God
who knows us by name.

We only get one life to steward.
One calling to answer.
One opportunity to live awake
to the riches secured for us in Christ.

Because we were not redeemed
with corruptible things,
such as silver or gold,
but with the precious blood of Christ,
a Lamb without blemish or spot.

We are here
to recognize the wealth
we now occupy
in this one life of salvation.

Because He called us out of uncertainty,
made us new,
and secured our destiny in Him,

We are here
to explore
the unsearchable riches in Christ
and to cast down every imagination
that attempts to rob us
of our heritage.

Because He does not need a Plan B,
and the end was settled from the beginning,

He ordered our steps,
prepared a table
in the presence of opposition,
and established victory
before the battle was seen.

We are here
to offer praise
for what has already been secured.

Because He brought us up and out,
so that we could serve Him,
this, too,
is a miracle.

He has been our portion.
He has increased us.
He has delivered us.

We cannot deny His hand.

We are here
to bless the name of the Lord
and declare:
the Lord lives.
Blessed be
the Rock of our salvation.

THAT'S WHY WE ARE HERE

Reflection

We Only Get One of These

Journal:

Write a prayer thanking God for the life you have been given and asking for wisdom to steward it with gratitude, faith, and surrender.

Scriptures:

1 Peter 1:18–19
Psalm 90:12

Make Request Known

Because we were bought with a sacrificial price,
and in the plan of salvation are invited
to come boldly and live elevated lives,
full of joy and peace,

We are here
to make our requests known,
to worship with confidence,
and to magnify
the name of the Lord.

Because He is the God of all flesh,
and nothing is too hard for Him,
today there is an answer
for an inquiring soul.

Make your request known.

Today there is healing
in prayer
for a wounded spirit.
Allow Him to minister.

Today there is increase in faith
for a listening ear.

We are here
to open our hearts,
our mouths,
and our hands,
allowing His love
to overflow.

Because we are passing through
in these earthen vessels,
and because He is raising a people,

We are here
to be tutored
in new speech,
a revelatory language.

We are learning
how to rename,
how to see,
how to believe,
how to pray,

how to live,
and how to seek
the Kingdom of God.

Because our spirit is ready,
and bears the glory of God,

We are ready
to hear what the Spirit
is saying to the church.

We are ready
to cast down imaginations
and every thought
that exalts itself
against the knowledge
we have come to receive.

We are here
to sharpen ear and heart,
so our hearing is clear,
our prayers unhindered,
and our praise uninterrupted,
as He ushers in
a new season.

THAT'S WHY WE ARE HERE

Reflection

Make Request Known

Journal:

Write a prayer making your request known to God.
Offer it in trust, thanking Him for His love, His power, and His faithfulness to meet you where you are.

Scripture:

Revelation 1:5

Sins Forgiven

Because one can still drown
by returning to sins already forgiven,
tugging at healed places,
resuscitating what no longer lives,
and exhausting breath
on matters that have been released.

Lifeless things
are not yoked
to abundant life.

And still, He remains the God of the breakthrough.

We are here to let forgiveness do its full work—
to release,
and to let God lead.

Forgiveness is complete.
We are not required to keep rebuilding the same cell.

Perhaps we have stood
holding a puzzling piece,
unsure where it belongs.

We are here
to trust the Master Builder
who knows the whole design,
understands our purpose,
and holds the final word.

In His skilled hands,
He may choose to:

- Refine what does not yet fit.
- Set something aside for the right time.
- Release what is nonessential.
- Elevate what truly adds value.

Because His thoughts toward us are good,
and He sees the full picture,

We are here
to acknowledge Him in all our ways,
to trust His direction,
and to give thanks.

 Forgiveness is complete.

We are done with prisons of our own making.
We need not live confined by
what God has already released.

Done with borrowed confinement.
Done living in timeouts
that He never assigned.

We are here
to know the Deliverer —
the One who opens doors
no one can shut.

We allow Him to:

- Create a clean heart.
- Renew a right spirit.
- Deposit treasures
and reveal great and mighty things.

Having been altered at the altar,

We are here
to gird our spirit with gladness,
to settle into righteousness,
and to clothe ourselves
with a garment of praise.

THAT'S WHY WE ARE HERE

Reflection

Sins Forgiven

Journal:

Write a prayer releasing what God has already released.
Thank Him for forgiveness that is complete, final, and freeing, and ask for grace to walk forward unburdened.

Scripture:

Micah 7:19

Melody in My Heart

Because when praise surrounds the heart,
it becomes a perimeter of protection,
unnecessary wounds
can no longer gain entry.
What once wounded the heart
now drowns
in the sound of praise.

He preserves us
with a song of deliverance.

We are here
to catch the melody,
to keep it in our hearts,
and to tune our minds
to what is virtuous
and worthy of praise.

Because He is a heart-fixer,
a body-healer,
and a restorer of the mind,

He has the power
to evict anything
that has taken up residence
without permission.

For the willing vessel,
the Healer is already present.

We are here
to approach His throne
with praise,
fully assured
that healing flows
and thanksgiving follows.

It is time to be healed.
It is time to occupy victory.

Because we are given one life,
and our days pass swiftly.

Why not thrive?

Riches and honor
come from Him.

What He blesses
is blessed indeed.

Whom the Son sets free
is free indeed.
We are here
to gain strength
to release
people, places, and things
that no longer serve His purpose.

The wilderness
is not our expected end.
The valley
is not our final dwelling.

He has rolled away reproach.

So instead of saying,
"This is the way I see it,"
with melody, we say,
"This is the day I see it."

Instead of saying,
"This is the way I am,"
we say,
"This is the day for I AM."

THAT'S WHY WE ARE HERE

Reflection

Melody in My Heart

Journal:

Write a prayer inviting God to retune your heart.
Ask Him to replace what no longer heals with a song of deliverance, peace, and freedom.

Scriptures:

Psalm 40:3
Isaiah 61:3

I Trust in You

Because trust placed in people can falter,
and certainty is never guaranteed,
but God watches over His Word
to perform it.
With Him, there is no hesitation.
No revision.
No uncertainty.

If trust was exercised this week,
if belief was put into motion,
we are here
to return exuberant praise
for calming restless waters
and for prayers answered.

Because the heart is an ignition,
it must be turned toward Him
to fully come alive.

If the inn of the heart
has become crowded
with uninvited guests,
movement slows.
Hearing dulls.
Willingness weakens.

So,
we are here to give notice,
releasing anything
that hinders trust,
anything that delays motion,
anything that keeps us
from moving from glory to glory.

We place our confidence in Him.
We rest our trust in Him.

THAT'S WHY WE ARE HERE

Reflection

I Trust in You.

Journal:

Write a prayer declaring your trust in God.
Release what has been crowding your heart and ask Him to renew your confidence in His faithfulness.

Scripture:

Proverbs 3:5–6

Power to Resist

Because what we do not resist
can quietly take root,
it begins to settle by consent,
leading to depletion,
complacency,
and deterioration.

Resistance is not striving—
it is refusing agreement
with what God did not plant.

But God does not deplete.

He fills.
He corrects.
He completes.
He perfects.

He is the Author
and the Finisher
of our faith.

We are here
to mature in Christ
and not resist
His good pleasure.

He desires to fill what is missing,
to complete what remains unfinished,
and to perfect
what concerns us.

Because He holds every answer,
we are invited
to resist lesser living—
and to remain alive in Christ.

So,
we seek the Lord
for His Word.

We allow it
to settle in the heart
and strengthen the spirit.

Joy and gladness
have not been cut off
from the house of the Lord.

Because He has drawn us out of many waters,
and we give Him full credit for His work,
today is a good day
to offer what is acceptable:

praise,
thanksgiving,
and worship.

We praise the name of the Lord
because He has dealt
wondrously with us.

And because He is perfecting
what He has entrusted to us,
we are here
to resist offenses,
to forgive those who have trespassed,
and to remain free
as He completes His work in us.

THAT'S WHY WE ARE HERE

Reflection

Power to Resist

Journal:

Write a prayer asking God to strengthen your heart, clarify your boundaries, and complete what He has already begun in you.

Scriptures:

James 4:7
Proverbs 4:23

Spiritual Growth & Reflection

An honest space for examining thought patterns, releasing hindrances, and allowing inner transformation to take root and flourish.

Appointments with Disappointments

When it feels like we are going the wrong way,
or when life tastes bitter
(Naomi comes to mind),
we are invited to stop—
not rush,
not pretend,
but inquire in His temple.

Some disappointments arrive
not as detours,
but as appointments—
moments where God meets us
before clarity returns.

What appears misdirected
may still be an appointment—
a moment God uses
before revealing the plan.

We are here to put on His strength.

There are destinations
not yet reached.
There is still territory to occupy.
The glory experienced at the destination
will overshadow the disappointment.

We are here to acknowledge Him
in all our ways,
so that He may direct our paths.

We overcome by inquiring in His temple,
asking for wisdom,
knowledge,
and direction.

When we release,
we will see peace.

Unforgiveness is like a hailstorm.
The longer one lingers in it,
the more damage is done.
It becomes a hindrance to the journey.

We are here to let go
and let God.

What is released
no longer weighs the steps.
What is surrendered
no longer governs the path.

We are here to learn wisdom
and refuse enticement
into what delays the journey.

THAT'S WHY WE ARE HERE

Reflection

Appointments with Disappointments

Journal:

Where have you recently felt disappointed, delayed, or misdirected?

What might God be developing or preparing in you through this season?

Is there anything you need to release in order to move forward in peace?

Scriptures:

Proverbs 3:5–6
James 1:5

Flesh, the Final Frontier

God placed us here
to do a work.

It is time to stop being robbed
in His house
by positioning what we know
or think we know
about each other
in front of the Word.

The flesh remains the final frontier—
the last place where reaction must yield to revelation,
and where the Spirit must govern response.

We were not called
to meditate on opinions
or to rehearse one another's failures
more than we rehearse
the promise of His return.

We are here to keep
the path to victory clear,
to increase in the knowledge of God,
so that we may continue to:

Walk worthy of the Lord
unto all pleasing,

Be fruitful in every good work,

Know and share
the hope of His calling.

At times, the outer layer of the flesh—
the final frontier of restraint—
is so primed
that the slightest friction
can ignite a blaze.

For the sake of righteousness
and self-preservation,
we are here to ask for perfect peace
and for wisdom,
so that our response
does not destroy our witness
or despise the covenant
we have with grace.

Sometimes revelation floods the heart
and creates an urgency
to move to higher ground.

We are here to look up,
not drown—
to be airlifted
by the Spirit of God,
lifted above reaction into discernment.
through a Word of transition.

Because our hope is in God.

He has been our healer.
He has been our deliverer.
He has been our way maker.

We are here to be introspective
at the frontier within,
and to inquire within:

"Why art thou cast down,
O my soul?"
"Why art thou disquieted
within me?"

Lest we forget—
God has been good to us.
Remember?
He parted our Red Sea.

We are here to command ourselves:
Awake, my soul.
Awake, my glory.
Make me hear joy and gladness.

Praise Him,
who is the health
of our countenance
and our God.

THAT'S WHY WE ARE HERE

Reflection

Flesh, the Final Frontier

Journal:

Where has your flesh been reacting faster than your spirit?

What response is the Spirit inviting you to bring into alignment with grace?

What would "higher ground" look like in your current situation?

Scriptures:

Psalm 42:5
Isaiah 26:3

Old Ruins

If we have spent the week
excavating old dirt ruins in our lives,
retrieving and turning over
ancient, broken cisterns,
that can no longer hold the water.

In the dawning of a new day,
we are here to explore
the richness of life in Christ,
to behold the new vessel
we have become,
and to keep that vessel
filled with living water.

Because if we can see it,
it is temporal.
It carries an expiration date.

We are here to pursue
spiritual things.
We are here to lay hold
of the hope of salvation
and to increase in faith.

Because we have seen
the hand of God before,
and we know—
God can, and God will.

We are here to walk by faith
and not by sight—
leaving old ruins behind
and living from what He has made new.

THAT'S WHY WE ARE HERE

Reflection

Old Ruins

Journal:

What old memory, habit, or pattern have you been revisiting that no longer sustains life?

What would it look like to keep your "new vessel" filled with living water this week?

Where is God inviting you to shift your focus from what is seen to what is eternal?

Scriptures:

2 Corinthians 5:17
Jeremiah 2:13

I Agree with God

Some people act out
simply because they can.

If we jump into someone else's
emotional cyclone,
it will not be long
before we are rung out
in their spin cycle.

Some situations are designed
to drain us,
interrupt our flow,
loosen our footing,
or test our restraint.

We are here to be loosed
from the need to know
what is wrong all the time.

We are here to gain strength,
keep the lights on,
and proceed into the liberty
to which we have been called.

We are here to agree with God—
not with constant diagnosis,
not with endless reaction.

For what is your life?
It is a vapor,
appearing for a moment,
then vanishing away.

Yet even in the diversity
of adversity,
He will not allow
our feet to be moved.

We are here as vessels of honor,
vessels of strength,
vessels of excellence,
carriers of His namesake,
and carriers of promise.

We are here:
to be examined for vulnerabilities,
to be strengthened with might

by the Spirit of the Living God,
to be strengthened through prayer.

Why?

Because His namesake matters.
And what is kept behind the veil—the inner life—must be guarded.

We agree with God:
He restores our soul.
He leads us in paths of righteousness
for His name's sake.

Fear can feel close,
but faith carries
a closer knowing
that He sees us
in adversity.

We are here for ever-increasing faith,
to abide under the shadow
of the Almighty,
and to grow in knowledge.

We agree with God:
that He would grant us,
according to the riches of His glory,
to be strengthened with might
by His Spirit
in the inner man.

THAT'S WHY WE ARE HERE

Reflection

Journal:

Write a short prayer of agreement with God—aligning your thoughts, reactions, and responses with His truth.

Name one area where you are choosing faith over reaction, restraint over impulse, and trust over control.

Scriptures:

Psalm 23:3
Ephesians 3:16

Stinking Thinking

Thinking the same thoughts all day
is like a dog chasing its tail—
circling endlessly, going nowhere fast,
yet convinced it is moving.

But when the thoughts are negative and unfruitful,
replayed not for minutes but for seasons,
they take us nowhere fast and leave us unhappy.

Sulking.
Gnawing.
Occupied as though something has possession of us.
We quietly forfeit what is already ours.

If we are going to be partakers in life,
we must be partakers of deliverance,
partakers of blessing,
partakers of new life,
partakers of joy that only God can give.

It is time—high time—for a new view.
Time to rise out of recycled thoughts
and move toward promised ground.

We cannot ascend carrying old bones.

We are here to choose:
the stale bone of yesterday,
or the richness, abundance, and vibrancy of life.

We are here to empty ourselves of what no longer serves purpose,
to ask forgiveness where we have been slow or slack,
and to stay focused—
determined not to be caught clutching what cannot nourish us.

Take flight.
New altitude requires new release.
Old baggage belongs at the altar, not in the cabin.

We are new creatures,
called to walk and speak in newness of life.

Spiritual awareness is why we are here.

Sometimes we overindulge the wrong emotions.
Too much worry becomes frustration.

Frustration becomes a hindrance.
Hindrances blur clarity,
interfere with freedom already paid for,
and weigh us down short of promise.

Unchecked thoughts eventually seek expression,
so renewal must begin in the mind.

We are here to propel—
not for personal spotlight,
but so He may be glorified.

It is not about us.
It is about Him.

Growth requires ascent.
Ascent requires release.
To become something new,
we must go higher.

We are here to receive His peace.
We are here for cleansing and release.
For the fervent prayers of the righteous still avail much.

THAT'S WHY WE ARE HERE

Reflection

Stinking Thinking

Journal:

Write one thought you need to let go of and one truth from God's Word you will intentionally take on.

Scripture:

Ephesians 4:23

Time for Expansion and to Flourish

Because it is time for expansion.
There is room.
There is unclaimed territory.

As we show God we are interested in a new thing,
there can be no room for captivity.

We are here to turn our backs to confinement,
turn our faces toward God,
arise, take up our bed, and walk.

Because it is also time to flourish.
And flourishing requires nourishment.

We are here
to seek Him earnestly,
to abide under the shadow of the Almighty,
to receive correction,
to receive instruction,
to lay up knowledge.

If we have received a Word to expand and flourish,
we are here to praise Him in advance
for His gentleness that makes us great,
for the new fragrance of growth,
for maturity forming in us,
for strength rising within us.

To the Immortal.
To the Invisible.
To the Infallible.
To the Incomparable—

We extend glad hearts
and give You glory, honor, and praise
for new residency in peace, prosperity, and growth.

THAT'S WHY WE ARE HERE

Reflection

Time for Expansion and to Flourish

Journal:

Name one area of expansion God is highlighting and one intentional step you will take to support growth there.

Scripture:

Isaiah 54:2

Praise and Worship

Reflections that return the heart to praise, trust, and reverence—rooted in remembrance of who God is and what He has done.

Seeking After God

In the storm, we sought after God
and found Him faithful to His Word.

He turned sorrow into joy.
He removed fear.
He restored trust.

We are here to thank Him
for meeting us in the storm
and changing the complexion of the situation.

Because we know
our transgressions have been forgiven,
our sins are covered,
and our footing is secure.

We are here to grow in grace
and in the knowledge of our Lord and Savior, Jesus Christ—
moving forward in what is good, acceptable,
and perfect in His will.

This season may carry pressure.

We are here to ask for
an extra measure of patience,
and grace toward others,
and for our responses to reflect Christ in us.

If we find ourselves resisting the Word,
or distracted by unnecessary contention,
we pause and realign—
choosing to receive rather than resist,
to meditate rather than debate,
to hear rather than harden.

Because God works beyond limits—
abundantly,
exceedingly,
and in the realm of "much more."

We are here to take limits off God
and ask Him where our feet should tread,
trusting that He has already commanded blessing
in a place called there—
the place of obedience where blessing is already assigned.

This is the day the Lord has made.
We will rejoice and be glad in it.

Even when burdens feel heavy,
we remember:
boulders were never designed for shoulders.

They weigh down the spirit
and obstruct the flow.

We are here to let go
and let God.

THAT'S WHY WE ARE HERE

Reflection

Seeking After God

Journal:

Write a short prayer surrendering one burden you've been holding.

Then note one simple, intentional way you will seek God this week, without pressure and without limits.

Scripture:

Matthew 6:33

He Knows, and He Holds

He knows, and He holds.
He knows what rests within our hearts.

Man looks on the outward appearance,
but God looks at the heart.

With all his possessions,
man eventually learns
there are things money cannot buy.

The outward requires resources.
The heart requires time with God.

So we pray,
"Lord, create in me a clean heart
and renew a right spirit within me."

Because if we are to draw
from the wells of salvation,
we desire to draw with clean hands—
Not only for ourselves,
but to strengthen one another,
for we do not always know
what another is carrying.

We are here for spiritual strengthening—
to set our posture
and incline ourselves.

We incline our eyes—
lifting them to the hills
from where our help comes.

We incline our understanding—
remembering that a way may seem right,
yet lead away from life.

We incline our ears—
knowing faith comes by hearing,
and hearing by the Word of God.
We incline our hearts—
hiding His Word within us
so it shapes how we live and walk.

He knows.
He holds.

THAT'S WHY WE ARE HERE

Reflection

He Knows, and He Holds

What part of my heart have I been guarding instead of offering to God?
How does knowing He holds me change the way I trust Him?

Journal:

Write a short prayer of surrender, offering God what He already knows.

Note one way you can intentionally make space this week to spend time with Him.

Scripture:

Psalm 139:1–2

His Testimonies Are Sure!

His testimonies are sure.
He has a proven record of lifting from pit to palace.

Because His testimonies are sure,
we keep our faces fully turned toward Him,
so we can recognize the path He is leading us on.

As we move forward, we are reminded:
the enemy does not always arrive as a roaring lion.
Sometimes he appears familiar—
in homes,
in relationships,
or even within self.

What does he seek?
To weaken resolve
until the will to fight fades.
To drain increase
and redirect it elsewhere.
To tamper with anointing
until light dims
and purpose loses sound.

But when distraction appears,
we stop —
look,
listen,
and keep our eyes forward,
and our ears tuned to the Lord.

Because when He says, "Well done,"
we will know that voice.
It will be unmistakable—
spoken to the just.

We are here to remain in right standing,
with upright hearts and forward motion.

Perfect peace is not elusive.
It is the fruit of trusting what God has already proven.
It is maintained through renewal —

In this kingdom,
He loads us daily with benefits.

So we respond.
We bring the fruit of our lips.
We praise Him who is the health of our countenance.
We praise Him
in whom we place all our trust.

THAT'S WHY WE ARE HERE

Reflection

His Testimonies Are Sure

Journal:

Write one testimony of God's faithfulness that comes to mind today.

Offer a prayer of praise, thanking Him for what He has done and for what He will yet do.

Scripture:

Psalm 19:7

Wonder How I Got Over?

Wonderful is in the wonder.
Even when we partially—
or entirely—
turned our backs,
He heard us
in the multitude of His mercy.

When our hearts failed diligence,
He strengthened them
and became our portion.

Even when we did not know
what the enemy was plotting,
He cut it off at the path.

He has shown Himself faithful.
We are here to show our gratitude.

"My lips shall greatly rejoice when I sing unto Thee,
and my soul which Thou hast redeemed."
He did not partially deliver us—
He brought us out fully.

We leave with full assurance
that what we asked
in the ears of the Lord of Hosts—
according to His will—will be honored.

Let the righteous be glad,
for He exalts the righteous.
Let us rejoice before our God.
Let us exceedingly rejoice.

Let us bless the Lord, our God.

THAT'S WHY WE ARE HERE

Reflection

Wonder How I Got Over

Where has God's hand clearly intervened—
bringing deliverance that could not have been achieved by effort alone?

Journal:

Record one moment of divine intervention.

Offer thanksgiving for God's faithfulness, both remembered and still unfolding.

Scripture:

Psalm 66:20

Oh, That Men Will Praise Him

Because I AM has blessed us, prospered us, straightened crooked places, and answered us,
we come with thankful hearts to serve the Lord with gladness.

No one entered alive in body and dead in spirit.
We came because we needed Him.
We came because we wanted Him.
We came because praise is our rightful response.

We are here to praise our way into His presence.

Through consecration, we learned that flesh can be denied,
and when it is, a well of living water springs up within us.

So we bless His name—not from habit, but from awakening.

Sometimes all that is required is a Word rightly received.
Yet an offense left unattended can dull reception.
So today, offenses are laid down,
the ear gate of the heart—
the place where truth is received and formed—
is opened,
and His Word is allowed to heal where healing is needed.

His truth still speaks.
It endures through every generation.
And because He is still speaking,
we choose to stay attentive—
to hear what the Spirit is saying to the church.

THAT'S WHY WE ARE HERE

Reflection

Oh, That Men Will Praise Him

Journal:

Where has my praise become restrained, delayed, or distracted?

Is there any offense, weariness, or familiarity dulling my gratitude?

What would it look like today to enter His presence again with gladness and thanksgiving?

Scripture:

Psalm 100:4–5

Reflection and Gratitude

A contemplative journey of looking back, giving thanks, and recognizing God's mercy, care, and sustaining presence across seasons.

Look Back Praise

Because our testimony can often be summed up in two words:
But God.

God is neither fickle nor stingy. His gifts are not afterthoughts.
He has been on our row, and we have been on His mind.
He has dealt with us in measures of exceeding abundance,
withholding no good thing.

We are here to give Him credit
and to praise Him for the unmistakable operation of His hand.

Grace installed a mirror in places we could not see.
Looking back, we now recognize moments that were not coincidence,
but pure grace—
grace that severed unhealthy ties,
grace that infused peace,
grace that positioned us to be presented faultless.

We are here to give look-back praise.

Because He has taught our hands to war,
He trained us to fight wisely—
delivering us from what once beset us
and rendering powerless what sought to hinder us.

We are here to pray, to ask for wisdom,
and to lift hands in prayer and surrender—without wrath, without doubt.

He has been our portion. He has given us a measure of faith.
And knowing that faith without works is dead,
we applied our hands with wisdom He supplied,
developed skill through His leading,
and pursued new avenues for increase.
He favored our work, and growth followed.

We are here to thank Him, remembering that He does the increasing and that faith is
meant to be lived.

THAT'S WHY WE ARE HERE

Reflection

Look Back Praise

Journal:

Reflect on a season where the outcome can only be explained by grace.

Where did God intervene, redirect, or protect you in ways you did not fully recognize at the time?

What skills, strength, or faith did He develop in you through that season?

Write a prayer or praise of thanksgiving, acknowledging His hand in your growth and deliverance.

Scripture:

Ephesians 3:2

Merciful God

Because God is our Daily Bread, and daily He loads us
with new mercies, new benefits,
showing forth His lovingkindness in the morning
and His faithfulness every night.

While breath and sound still remain,
mercy still calls forth a resounding YES.

We are still here—
living, walking in obedience,
sowing seeds that outlive the moment.

We are here with joy and gladness of heart
for the abundance of things the Lord has done for us.

Because He knows how to conceal our matters
while revealing His secrets,
we are confident that what we placed
in the ears of the Lord of Sabaoth
has been healed and sealed
in the womb of Peace and Truth.

Since His Word declares
He will never leave us nor forsake us,
we rest knowing:

He is Sovereign.
He scatters and gathers.
He knows when to give
and when to burn off what does not belong.

We are here to rest what remains with Him
and to bless His holy name.

He is the great coordinator of just-in-time provision.
He has been our bridge over troubled waters.
He cut off enemies
and transformed lack into prosperity.

We are here to give thanks to the great Problem Solver,
mindful of the promises whispered
in seasons of trouble.

Because we do not have to wait for the end of time
to worship and know God,
even as we journey onward.

We are here to enter His gates with thanksgiving,
enter His courts with praise,
be thankful unto Him,
and bless His name.

For the Lord is good.
His mercy is everlasting.
His truth endures to all generations.

THAT'S WHY WE ARE HERE

Reflection

Merciful God

Journal:

Where has God's mercy been evident in daily life rather than only in major moments?

What has been given, removed, protected, or timed with care for good?

Write a prayer of thanksgiving, acknowledging mercy not only in what was received, but also in what was lovingly withheld.

Scripture:

Psalm 59:16

His Universe

We do not anchor our faith
in human theories
concerning how the universe was formed.

The mind of man cannot fully comprehend
the beauty he cannot recreate,
nor exhaust the laws he did not author.
Some things will remain mystery
long after we become ancestors.

We believe simply and securely:
In the beginning—God.

And under His lets—His permissions and order—we thrive.

We are here to praise Him
for the statute, authority,
and dominion He has entrusted to us.

Because this week was not surrendered
to constant enter-take-ment—
those influences that quietly shape the mind—
but instead to prayer, meditation,
and the reading of His Word,

We have seen fruit:

He has caused us to inherit
the labor of others.
We have seen the goodness of the Lord
in the land of the living.

We are here to thank Him
for a renewed mind
and for prospering our way.

For every time we turned back toward Him,
every time we turned our attention to God,
every time we prayed,
fasted,
exalted His name,
or entered worship—

He continued to bless us,
again and again.
So—
we are here to bless His name.

We are here to offer our lives,
and our praise,
to the Lord.

THAT'S WHY WE ARE HERE

Reflection

His Universe

Journal:

Where has God's order, peace, or blessing emerged when His presence was chosen over distraction?

Reflect on one moment when turning attention toward God renewed the mind or shifted perspective.

Write a brief prayer of gratitude, acknowledging Him as Creator, Sustainer, and the One who orders your way.

Scripture:

Genesis 1:26

The Thicket of Flesh

Perhaps something became caught
in the thicket of one's attention.

Instead of releasing it,
it was handled, revisited, wrestled with,
and rehearsed—
until attention fed it enough
to grow larger than intended.

Since our desire is to draw closer,
we are here to pray for the renewing of the mind,
for the strength to open the trap,
let the issue go free,
and give that space back to the Lord.

An issue is temporary.
It will not follow us into eternity.
If it is disturbing peace,
we are here to place it under the Blood,
where forgiveness covers,
freedom is secured,
and we move forward.

We praise God in advance
for a peaceful place.

Bondage tightens.
Entanglements entangle.
Strongholds hold fast.

Why heap sorrow upon tomorrow?
There is no more time for this.

We are here to be disentangled,
empowered to stand,
and to walk in the liberty
unto which we were called.

Issues placed in a flesh-pot—
shared, rehearsed, and circulated through conversation
tend to multiply and scatter.

Issues placed in the Master's hands
are handled with wisdom.
So we learn how to cast
if we are going to last.

Because He desires that we prosper
and be in good health,
even as our soul prospers—
a soul saturated with joy and peace.

He has greater on His mind,
while we have distractions on ours.

So we declare:

Humdrum, your rhythm ends here.
Worry, your welcome has expired.
Doubt, you will no longer cripple.
Self, release the weight of other people's storms.

We are here to release
and to praise the One who came
that we might have life,
and have it more abundantly.

THAT'S WHY WE ARE HERE

Reflection

The Thicket of Flesh

Journal:

Where might God be inviting you to release it fully—so that peace, clarity, and freedom can take its place?

Write a prayer of surrender, placing this matter back into God's care and asking for wisdom to walk forward unburdened.

Scriptures:

Romans 12:2
Ephesians 4:23–24

God of Comfort

Because He sits high and looks low,
He knows when one needs to move
from a hug
to being held.
And if one desires to be held,
He is the Great Comforter.

We are here to find comfort in His words
and to incline into Him,
as no one else can—

hold you,
hold onto you,
love you,
rock you,
rest you,
and bless you —
like Father God.

We are not here to rush past His presence
to adore things made of fiber, plastic, leather,
wood, stone, or stubble—
things that cannot comfort the soul.

We are here because He has already proven Himself.

He ransomed us.
He forgave our sins.
He answered our prayers.
He quieted raging storms
and restored us with honor.

We are here to respond with grateful hearts.

Because sometimes, without warning,
an ill word is spoken—
facts unknown,
venom released.

It lodges in the flesh,
disturbs the spirit,
steals rest,
and tries to rewrite the conversation.

But the thief will not have the final word.
We are here to ensure our foundation is strong enough

for nonsense to roll off
and for intended harm
to become a non-event.

Perhaps there is a need:
for estrangement from lust,
for family wounds to be healed,
for a life-changing Word,
or for stolen glory to be restored.

The King has sent His Word.

Who is this King of glory?
The Lord—strong and mighty,
the Lord—mighty in battle.

He is the great Mind Regulator.
He is the Great Reconciler.

We are here to receive our healing,
our answer,
and our comfort—
and to advance to higher ground
with singleness of vision
and a spirit made whole.

THAT'S WHY WE ARE HERE

Reflection

God of Comfort

Journal:

Where has there been a need not just for help—but for holding?

What has tried to disturb your peace recently, and how might God be inviting rest instead of replaying the wound?

Write a prayer releasing what has weighed on your heart and welcoming God's quieting presence.

Scripture:

Zephaniah 3:17

Watered Garden

Because we have a Deliverer in the matter
and understanding lives within us,
we know we have a right to be free.

Chains are not comely on the righteous.
The righteous are meant to flourish.

We are here to shake loose anything
that clogs the flow
and impedes the greatness God intends.

Because we have been proving
what is good, acceptable, and perfect in His will,
and refusing to dwell in lukewarm places
that dull the spirit.

The only gifts befitting our King
are lives laid down
and praise lifted up before Him.

Because He transplanted a wounded soul
into a watered garden
and steered us into paths of righteousness.
Because He continually causes us
to flourish and triumph in His hands.

We are here to bow down,
declare His goodness,
and let the voice of His praise be heard.

Since our hope rests
in a resurrected Savior—
our Defense,
our Rock,
our Refuge,
our Rest—

We are here to increase in faith
through continual intake of the Word of God.

Because He is the great Coordinator
of just-in-time provision.
He has been our bridge
over troubled waters.
He cut off enemies
and transformed lack into prosperity.

He did not remove opposition
before His glory was seen.
He prepared a table in their presence—
a table filled with peace,
victorious speech,
blessed assurance,
and fresh oil,
all for His glory.

We are here to praise the Lord for victory
and to become instruments of praise.

Because prayer solved the equation
and praise reduced it
to healing and wholeness,
we are here to give thanks
to the great Problem Solver.

THAT'S WHY WE ARE HERE

Reflection

Watered Garden

Journal:

Where has God restored what was once wounded or dry in your life?

What practices help keep your soul watered and flourishing, rather than simply surviving?

Write a brief prayer, thanking God for where He has planted you and asking for grace to continue growing in righteousness and peace.

Scriptures:

Proverbs 11:28
Isaiah 58:11

Ready to Release and Unleash

What can we render to the Lord
for all His benefits toward us?

If we were to pour out an offering today—
not from our hands, but from our hearts—
what would it contain?

We are not speaking of a reasonable portion.
Our most valuable contents cannot be measured,
contained, or confined.

They are carried within vessels shaped by grace,
rekindled by mercy,
and strengthened by faith.

We remember:
We are no longer confined to condemnation.
He met us in wilderness places.
He made a way of escape.
He removed hindrances and blockages.
He caught us when we were spiraling.
Grace and mercy never left our camp.
He restored health to our countenance
and became our sustaining strength.
He gave rest on every side.
He compounded blessings upon blessings.
He attended to the voice of our prayers.
He set plans in motion that extend beyond us.

The contents are not light.
They are not empty.

Since we came into His presence ready to release,
we are here to unleash
a heart full of thanksgiving
and a mouth full of praise.

It is our privilege to bless His name.

How do we bless the One
whose Spirit hovered over the deep
and brought order from chaos?

The One who stretched out the heavens,
formed the earth,
and breathed life into mortal bodies.

The One who is Almighty,
Sovereign, Eternal, Faithful, Refuge,
Comforter, Portion, and Creator.

Thine, O Lord, is the greatness,
the power, the glory,
the victory,
and the majesty.
All that is in heaven and earth is Yours.
You are exalted as Head above all.

We are not here to retire on grace.
We are seasoned for a reason —
prepared for the work this season requires.

After receiving from the well,
we are here to pour back into the earth.
After being filled,
we are here to flow.

Seated in Him,
we think positionally.
We are complete in Him.
Above and not beneath.
Heirs and joint heirs.
Called unto righteousness.

We are here to be renewed
in the spirit of our minds
and to respond to life
from the position He has already given us.

THAT'S WHY WE ARE HERE

Reflection

Ready to Release and Unleash

Journal:

What has God filled you with that is meant to be poured out?

Write one way you will intentionally release gratitude, testimony, or service this week.

Scripture:

1 Chronicles 29:11–12

Reflection

www.ingramcontent.com/pod-product-compliance
Lightning Source LLC
Chambersburg PA
CBHW040907130726
48005CB00019BA/3004